STOP STOPPING YOUR FORTUNE

SIX RULES FOR HAPINESS

L. J. PAUMAN

STOP STOPPING YOUR FORTUNE

TABLE OF CONTENTS

I dedicate this book to my wife Suzana, my son Tadej and my daughter Natalija.

PREFACE

Many books and thoughts are written about spirituality and happiness. They interpret and advise us how to live and achieve happiness and satisfaction in life. However, it is very difficult for us to achieve it in practice and accept, follow and do, what they advise.

The aim of my writing is in a short and concise way to collect the things that are written in a variety of books, old writings, sayings, stories. They are generally known to most people, but in everyday life they are not realized and used.

I found out, that all these lessons can be collected into six rules which will help us in different life situations to overcome difficulties and gradually achieve happiness and fortune.

The point is not just to read the book and then put it aside. The book should serve as a guide to us, or a kind of instruction manual of our life. It contains everything we need. We just need to find the right thing and stick to it.

Each chapter, which deals with one rule, consists from some important sayings that confirm it, from short explanations and tips on how to use it in everyday life, some carefully selected short stories, which the best provides us with certain life lessons helping us to solve specific problems and direct us to reconsider why certain things happen in our lives and how to act in certain situations. There are listed some positive affirmations which we can use to focus our thoughts to positive thinking, which will consequently lead to the achievement of our goals in life.

Our daily mission is to change our negative thought patterns, keeping to the rules and consequently make our life easier.

Let's try to find out what is our life mission and what is the most important to learn in our life. We should ask ourselves, whether we have already learned the values which remain our greatest wealth that can't be stolen or lost and can be always carried with us. Have we improved our character enough, learned compassion, forgiveness, understanding and got rid of hatred, resentment, evil and fear? Have we already overcome the sins and instincts that bring misfortune and malaise to us and to people in our surroundings, such as anger, fear, laziness, envy, gluttony, greed, lust, depression, vanity, attachment? These are the so-called head sins. It means that they cause problems to those who had created them in their head with their thoughts.

By understanding of our daily problems and the knowledge of how to live properly and how to use the self-healing method, we can make our lives easier and find shortcuts to our life goals and fortune. We will achieve it by using and respecting the rules and advices in this book. Everything we need is inside this book.

INTRODUCTION

I have decided to write a book that will enable people to achieve happier life, more understanding to each other and consequently make a better world. The aim of my writing is to collect, more precisely, thoughts and lessons that can help people to achieve a higher quality of life, happiness, comfort, consolation or support to begin to recognize and understand why certain bad or good events are happening. We must realize that, if we succeed in our life transfer only one good property to another person, for example on our child, it will touch all people in a few hundred years. Therefore, it is pointless to moan that we, as individuals, have no influence on the world and people. The fact is, that everyone will a specific positive property or knowledge that helps him in life transfer on to their descendants.

The fact is that we are not the absolute owners of our lives. We didn't create ourselves. We do not have any influence on the time of our birth or death. Accordingly, there must exist a force that has created us and has enabled our existence in the current form, because we do not have this capability. It is not important what it is called or god, a creator, life energy, evolution, nature or force. It is important that we should all our prayers and wishes direct to this force to help us. If it had the power to enable our current existence, then undoubtedly also has the ability to support us and help us with our daily problems and fulfil our requests and desires.

The true faith has the one who has reached a level in his life, believing that all things in life happen to him in his own good, no matter if they are good or bad.

It is difficult to believe that at a specific moment a bad thing, like an accident, a loss of job or death in the family is good for us and our development. We can namely at a particular moment see the tragedy clearly ahead.

However, those who have a true faith and trust in the force that had created them will consider a specific event good for their development, although they will not find any logical explanation for the specific situation.

The event can be compared with a cut from the film. We can see only a current picture on the film, but our creator can see the entire movie. For comparison, we can take the situation with babies who are crying and are angry when taking a bath. Although we know that this is good for them, they are not aware of that, because they have in mind only their current discomfort and possess no consciousness to understand the situation.

In our life we often behave similarly. If we truly have trust and faith in the force that enables our existence, then each anger and sadness is totally unnecessary. Why should we get angry for little things, if we knew that in the long term they are good for us? Imagine how sad and angry was a man who lost the ticket for the Titanic, and how happy was a man who got it.

We are often angry, because we are under time pressure and we are late for a few minutes, even though, because of our punctuality, we might have been involved in a car accident. We must realize that we have no awareness and senses that allow us a full view. We are unable to decide what is good for us, because we do not have access to the whole movie.

We're namely restricted with our five senses, which are for us in fact the cage in which is caught our soul. There exist in the universe and around us a lot more things than we are able to perceive with our senses. Let us imagine how powerful we would consider a creature that has one sense more than we- the sixth sense. Wouldn't we be powerful in comparison to others, if we were the only in the world with the sense of smell? Then the others would wonder how, for example, we know that the neighbours are cooking.

When we die, we become free from the limitations of our five senses and achieve a level of consciousness that allows us to view the entire "movie". Our brain is just the means that allows our consciousness to operate within the frame of our five senses and takes care of our physical functions, while our real essence is far more than our temporary physical body.

There are people who had experienced a near death experience and were later able to predict future events. It is possible that they had an insight into the whole "movie" or a part of it, because they were no longer limited within the senses of their physical body.

Shakespeare wrote in Hamlet: "There are more things in heaven and earth, than are dreamt of in your philosophy." The meaning of life is that we, at our current stage of consciousness, learn something. All individuals have their own destiny and are pushed into life situations that match to their "education program" that will lead them to certain conclusions and consequently to higher consciousness.

Therefore, there exist differences between people, and each has its own program of "education". Our task is to carry out that education in the best possible way and with the minimum of possible problems. We can also for help recall the old proverb: "A fool learns on their own experiences, but the wise on foreign". However, it is very difficult to learn from foreign experience, because what we feel on our own skin more efficiently contributes to the maturing of our personality.

I once saw a car with a sticker on the back with the inscription: "I trust my Creator, and therefore I do not need additional insurance". A person with such opinion believes that everything what might happen is good for him and his personal development. If all people believed that, then the insurance companies would be out of their work.

To change our view on the events in our life is essential to achieve happiness. There is no more reason for the anger, which is a negative emotion that brings us misfortune, and takes our energy.

Anger and fear are the main emotions that hinder us from achieving happiness and satisfaction in life.

Fear is our worst enemy, which attracts negative forces. Comparison can be found in the animal world. Beasts attack those animals which are weak or show fear. A dog will attack the person who is afraid of it.

From our own experience we know, that bad things are happening more often just to those people who are afraid of certain things. Car accidents are happening more often to those who are afraid of driving, or are concerned about their new car. Money will lose those who have the greatest fear of loss. The disease has affected just the one, who had had the greatest fear of it. Often happen to us those things that we expect the worst.

It happens, however, also the opposite. Women in some primitive tribes do not feel pain in childbirth for the simple reason, because they are not afraid of it. Why some people are constantly undergoing the same or similar bad things or events? The main cause is the fear in the background. We must overcome it and then we will be able to live normally.

For all the things that happen to us, we should blame only ourselves. First, it is necessary to change ourselves and, consequently, the others will change their relationship to us. We will start to attract different events and people, and consequently different things and situations are going to happen to us. The point is, that we will have to recognize why certain things happen to us and what the force, which has enabled our existence, wants to teach us.

Each disease has a psychic cause in the background. We get sick because of our negative thinking and expectations. Everyday stress, lack of a feeling of security, fear, worries, distrust, disappointment, anger and resentment is the cause that our subconscious mind is trying to find a solution and creates a disease on the physical level.

For example, we get sick and we do not need to go to work. Our subconscious mind has created a short-term solution that would save us from problems at work. The subconscious mind is a tool of our consciousness, which listens to a stronger master. Will the stronger be the fear of failure, or belief in success? That what will be stronger will prevail and effect on the outcome of the event.

Even the official medicine and science increasingly realize that the emotional background may be the main cause of the disease. More and more literature can be found on the topic of positive thinking. Thought is a force or energy that creates and influences events in our future. Each thought tends to materialize. In the Bible, it is written that the first was the word, or thought. The scientist would prefer the word information.

Visualization is becoming increasingly useful method for achieving certain goals. The proofs of the power of the psyche are schizophrenia, hypnosis and stigmas. It means that the thought has such power that can cause changes in the physical level. Similarly, can be explained various miraculous healings.

How works the connection and relation between our subconscious mind and our creator we are not able to understand. Just like we are not able to understand the concept of eternity and infinity, or imagine the reality in more than three dimensions or how the universe began.

We are in fact limited by our five senses and our mind, just as a computer with less power that is not capable to handle large-scale data. In the same way there exist the differences in the consciousness and perceptions between the living creatures, including human beings, animals and plants.

Interesting are the new discoveries about plants. Namely, that just like people, they can feel, have a memory and are aware of the differences between good and bad and even can perceive other beings over longer distances. So, brain and senses that we know are not the only means and condition for intellect, perception and consciousness.

All living beings are related to each other at a certain level. They are connected by a force for which are used a variety of terms such as a creator, nature, universal intelligence, energy or god.

We know a lot of expressions to compare the relationship between that power and an individual like: "God is the ocean - a man is the wave, God is a tree - a man is a leaf, God is the central computer - a man is a terminal, God is the sun - a man is a sunbeam.

People are in their essence spiritual beings. The world we perceive is probably only a hologram or illusion, created by our brain. The reality is far greater than the three-dimensional world that we can see. Every living being perceives the world in many different ways, depending on the limitations of the body and the brain. What is the true reality is not known to us. Scientists presume that the universe mainly consists of the substance called dark matter, which we can't perceive.

After death, when we get rid of the limitations of our material body, we become aware of our essence. We can also say that we return to the creator and become a part of it. A part of which we have always been, but we are not aware of that, because we are convinced in our ego. We behave like a wave in the ocean, which trembles before its neutralizing.

The human body is like a vehicle and our soul is like a driver, which is at the level of consciousness, as it allows its material body.

Our fate is like the route by which we drive. The route may be straight, winding, clear or unclear. In any case, we can see only a limited distance ahead of us. Only if our consciousness rose up above the vehicle – body, we could see the entire route.

Our life is like a journey. We have free will how to avoid certain obstacles on our way. If we know the driving rules and consider them, then our driving will be safer, more comfortable, easier, and we will easily achieve our goals.

We can also use shortcuts. Why would we choose a more difficult path if exists an easier one? There are also obstacles on our way and situations to which can't be influenced and also the end is not known.

6 RULES FOR HAPPY LIFE

People in their life haven't got any instructions for that how to live to achieve happiness. Any machine we buy has got the instructions for use, but people haven't got any. Buddhists say that the luck must be built, rather than wait for it.

With knowing how to live properly, we can facilitate and ease our life and find shortcuts to our goals. We can achieve it by using the following rules, which are in fact universal laws, which can be also found in various religions, old writings and sayings. It works the same as in the traffic. The more we consider the traffic signs and traffic rules, the lower will be possibility of involving into an accident. When it is too late does not help any excuse that we did not know the rules.

Rule number 1

Think positively

Everything is inside me

In our physical life, our subconscious mind has the task that it materializes everything in what we believe strongly enough. It will happen to us what we expect. The subconscious mind obeys the stronger master. The question is, whether the stronger the fear is, or our positive expectations. The subconscious mind has all the information, also how to heal our bodies.

Creative power is within us. Our spirit and mind can control matter. Our thoughts can create miracles. The only restriction is our limited way of thinking. We can create everything what we believe hard enough, but there shouldn't be present any doubt at all.

Visualization is the best self-healing method

I suggest visualization for the best self-healing method. This means that we create in our mind a picture of the future, how we will be healthy again, or how a particular event is going to be realized. That picture we constantly imagine.

The best way is to perform it every night before going to sleep, because so it is easier to influence on our subconscious mind. The same as you can order yourself in the evening at exactly what time to wake up in the morning, without looking at the clock, so can our subconscious mind ensure that our expected figure realizes in the future. We can also determine the time when the change enters. Before bedtime, we can order ourselves that when we wake up in the morning, our health and feeling will be much better. Overnight the healing process will begin and our health will become constantly better, all the way to the full recovery.

Be aware, however, that the disease did not occur overnight, the same way our body also uses its time until it comes to a cure. The most important thing is that we have the subconscious mind focused on healing.

Positive or negative thoughts influence on our physical body

Energy is flowing to the location where we focus our attention. Namely, the thing in which we invest too much energy insists. The solution is that we begin to emit new changes through positive thinking and focus the attention from disease into health, from a lack into wealth, from sorrow into joy, from bad into good, from fear into courage, from anger into tolerance.

Even the newest research in the field of quantum physics shows that there are particles much smaller than atoms that exist in an undefined state and take a certain shape only when they are affected by consciousness that observes them. Amazing evidence of the power of thought can be seen in hypnosis or certain mental illnesses such as schizophrenia and hysteria.

In the case of hysteria people can be observed who are paralyzed, but after a few hours they may be perfectly normal, and vice versa.

In schizophrenia, a person with multiple personalities may suffer from different diseases, depending on the personality, which is a certain time in the foreground.

Hypnosis is another example, where we can see what hidden power lies in a man and how powerful is the influence of thoughts on the subconscious mind and physical body. A hypnotized person can get the body so hard that you can walk on it when lying between two chairs, or can perfectly well read the text, although in its normal state needs glasses.

In the same way, we can use positive or negative thoughts to influence on our physical body to experience positive or negative changes. This means that you can cure a particular disease, or create it with negative thinking. Therefore, it is very important, what our thoughts are.

One day in the future being sick will be a shame, because there will be generally considered the fact that the cause of the disease is negative thinking.

What group do you belong to?

What is the difference between a person who thinks positively and a person who thinks negatively? To which group do you belong?

For example, the person who looks negatively on the world would by observing children at play see first the threats, or damage that might be caused.

Opposite of that, positively directed person would see the joy of children at play first.

In practice, the most difficult thing is to replace negative thought patterns with positive ones. Very quickly people get used to watch the world with care and fear, but it is difficult to do it contrary. If you do not want to be constantly embittered and in constant fear of what will happen bad, it is necessary immediately start changing your thought patterns.

Changing our thought patterns

This can be done in the following steps:

1. We must become constantly aware of our negative thoughts.

2. When we recognize a negative thought, immediately stop thinking it to the end.

3. We replace the negative thought with a positive or at least neutral one.

4. Our attention must be given to something what will provoke pleasant feelings.

Let's become a magnet for positive events

Let us have constantly prepared some positive thoughts that will serve as alternative thoughts. We can prepare them in the morning when we wake up, or before going to bed for the next day. If we find a new positive thought we prepare it for an alternative thought. If we consistently stick to this advice, we will gradually begin to change our thought patterns until we automatically think positively. Consequently, in this way we will reduce the ability to call up bad events. We will become a magnet for positive events.

We attract what we think about

When we set the vision, we must put a clear affirmation. It is important to think about health or money, not the lack of it. We attract what we think about something. If we think about the lack of something, we will namely attract lack. If we think and act positive, we will also attract into our lives good people, circumstances and events.

We must get rid of all the dark thoughts that relate to other people. If we think and expect about other people only the worst, then we transmit the negative energy which also likely provokes such behavior in them, as we expected.

With positive thinking and expectations, we create a field that attracts premonitions and coincidences that will help us. It is important that when we notice that our attention is paid to something that raises negative emotions in us, then we must immediately focus our attention to something else, to anything that will provoke in us pleasant feelings.

When we feel well, then we emit friendly vibrations and the universe must bring things that delight us.

Our negative thoughts can attract the curse to us or to others, so we have to get rid of reflections and the use of words such as: I'm worried about the future ..., I do not have money ..., I cannot afford that ..., I am not able..., it will harm me..., I cannot get out of debt..., I don't deserve that..., always happen bad things to me, it's hard to..., I am going to fail..., I do not go on dates..., I always have problems..., life is cruel, I'm afraid, also smoking is killing you.

These are dangerous thoughts, so called curses, which tend to realization and materialization. In any case, we should avoid thoughts, words and affirmations like that.

We must focus on the abundance in our life, so our thoughts and words must be replaced with positive, such as: I can do that, I can afford that..., it makes me happy..., I will succeed..., everything is taking place in my own good ..., I have enough money ..., it is going to be easy for me..., I know that at the moment I am receiving, the universe supports me in everything, I'm doing it well.

Switching to positive thoughts

Find out the number of the negative thoughts in a certain period of time. Throughout the day we mark the number of negative thoughts with black dots on a paper. At the end of the day we count the number. The next day, we try to reduce the number of them. We repeat the procedure every day, so long, that we change our thought patterns. Consequently, we'll begin switching to positive thoughts automatically.

Let's learn from these short stories!

In the Paradise
(Author Unknown)

One man was travelling and suddenly he got to the paradise.

He sat down under the desire tree (there is such tree in the paradise, sitting under which you can immediately fulfil any your desire, you just need to think about it) and thought: "I am hungry, so it would be nice to have a bite right now." And when he just thought about this, a table full of different dishes that he was thinking about appeared right before him.

Wow! – The man was surprised, – but it can't be! – He thought so, and the table with dishes disappeared immediately. "It would be nice to get it back!" – And dishes appeared again.

He ate a plenty of dishes – he has never eaten such tasty food before. After satisfying hunger he thought: it would be nice to drink something – and a perfect wine appeared immediately, because there are no restrictions in the paradise.

Lying in the shadow of the tree and drinking wine, he started wondering: Why these miracles do happen? It just can't be that everything would be so good – probably some ghosts played a joke on me.

Suddenly the ghosts appeared. They were terrible and looked like he imagined them.

The man became scared and thought: now they will kill me!

And they killed him.

The lesson of the story:
Everyone lives in the world that he deserves. Everyone attracts what he thinks about.

In a Deep Pit

(Author Unknown)

As a group of frogs were traveling through the woods, two of them fell into a deep pit. When the other frogs crowded around the pit and saw how deep it was, they told the two frogs that there was no hope left for them.

However, the two frogs decided to ignore what the others were saying and they proceeded to try and jump out of the pit. Despite their efforts, the group of frogs at the top of the pit were still saying that they should just give up. That they would never make it out.

Eventually, one of the frogs took heed to what the others were saying and he gave up, falling down to his death. The other frog continued to jump as hard as he could. Again, the crowd of frogs yelled at him to stop the pain and just die.

He jumped even harder and finally made it out. When he got out, the other frogs said, "Did you not hear us?"

The frog explained to them that he was deaf. He thought they were encouraging him the entire time.

The lesson of the story:
Our thoughts have a great influence on the outcome. People's words can have a big effect on other's lives. Let us not always listen to the words of failure

On the Rope
(Author Unknown)

As a man was passing the elephants, he suddenly stopped, confused by the fact that these huge creatures were being held by only a small rope tied to their front leg. No chains, no cages. It was obvious that the elephants could, at any time, break away from their bonds but for some reason, they did not.

He saw a trainer nearby and asked why these animals just stood there and made no attempt to get away. "Well," trainer said, "when they are very young and much smaller we use the same size rope to tie them and, at that age, it's enough to hold them. As they grow up, they are conditioned to believe they cannot break away. They believe the rope can still hold them, so they never try to break free."

The man was amazed. These animals could at any time break free from their bonds but because they believed they couldn't, they were stuck right where they were.

The lesson of the story:
Like the elephants, how many of us go through life hanging onto a belief that we cannot do something. Simply because we failed at it once before. Failure is a part of learning. We should never give up the struggle in life.

Optimist and Pessimist
(Author Unknown)

There is a story of identical twins. One was a hope-filled optimist. "Everything is coming up roses!" he would say. The other twin was a sad and hopeless pessimist. He thought that Murphy, as in Murphy's

Law, was an optimist. The worried parents of the boys brought them to the local psychologist.

He suggested to the parents a plan to balance the twins" personalities. "On their next birthday, put them in separate rooms to open their gifts. Give the pessimist the best toys you can afford, and give the optimist a box of manure." The parents followed these instructions and carefully observed the results.

When they peeked in on the pessimist, they heard him audibly complaining, "I don't like the colour of this computer... I'll bet this calculator will break ... I don't like the game ... I know someone who's got a bigger toy car than this ..."

Tiptoeing across the corridor, the parents peeked in and saw their little optimist gleefully throwing the manure up in the air. He was giggling. "You can't fool me! Where there's this much manure, there's got to be a pony!"

The lesson of the story:
It's very hard to change your character. But we must learn to become positive.

Remember these sayings!

Think and work joyfully and you'll feel that way.

*

We are experiencing what we think.

*

Joy is the energy that responds to our expectations.

*

Heaven is within us.

*

When the idea is born, it tends to the realization and materialization.

*

Our life is the product of our thoughts

Rule number 2

What does not destroy me makes me stronger

A fool learns from its own experience, but the wise man from others

People often stigmatize the others saying, "That one is incompetent, an alcoholic, a divorcee or a spender". But the sentence could be configured differently and we can say that this is a person who has got experience with alcohol, experience with separation and experience with failure or loss. Then we should realize that we are dealing with a person who has significant experience or knowledge on this matter.

We have no right to condemn such a person and we can learn a lot from it. But usually people decide to learn on more difficult way, because what we experience on our own skin works more efficiently. That confirms a saying that a fool learns from its own experience, but the wise man from others.

We must learn to withstand failures and defeats and learn from them

We can easily withstand the success, but it is difficult to withstand the failure. Even the weakest person will easily withstand a success. But it is difficult on the contrary. Only the most solid and stable personality withstands greater defeats. Therefore, we should not be disappointed with the defeat. This is only the school of life, which helps us to maturation of our personality. We must learn to withstand failures and defeats and learn from them.

If there occurred constantly successes in life, then the very first smallest failure would break us. Namely we would not have the experience and the strength to overcome it.

Problem solving by itself helps to the maturation of personality. Only those people, who experienced failures themselves, would have useful experience to help others and themselves in similar situations.

There were people who had achieved wealth, prestige, power and high social status, but sudden failure and loss broke them down. They have committed suicide. Although, they could have found a different solution. Those people, who must be regularly confronted with the shortage, financial difficulties, their survival, humiliations, would not fall in despair and even think of committing suicide. To the end of their life, they would be fighting, gaining experiences and consolidating their personality, although they would never reach a significant social status. Statistically higher percentage of suicides is committed in countries with a higher social standard. Remember that when you lose, you gain the lesson.

Every problem will repeat until we are ready to face it and will be solved

If there an afterlife and reincarnation exist, then it is logical, that in the next life, we will be confronted again before a similar, or even more severe, situation. The problem will repeat until we are ready to face it and will be solved. When our physical death was a definite end of existence, then we would never have to answer for all our sins. But that is not logical, because we would not suffer any punishment for all our sins and we could do whatever we want, even bad things. Consequently, people would not need to strive to become better. There also would be no explanation to the question why people are born in different social environments, because logically, there should be equal opportunities for all.

It makes more sense, that after our physical death, our life in some form continues and so every individual within a certain period of life and time pays for all his sins. Once the actor Woody Allen made a joke saying, that he would like to commit suicide, but with his bad luck, it would be only a short-term solution.

If all our consciousness, all the emotions, all the suffering and joy, all beautiful and bad memories are hidden in a few square centimetres of meat somewhere between the ears, then the meaning of our life absurd. If our brains are the only center, where are saved all our memories, emotions, consciousness, then also we do not have anything to worry about what will happen after death. It also means, that no judgment, punishment, suffering or new opportunity is going to happen to us, and we will end up all the same, regardless of the good or bad works in our lives. So it does not matter whether we are good or bad, because the end is the same for everyone. But our experience shows, that it is not logical, that everything has the same end, but that consequences are different and depend on actions in the past.

Maybe in the future scientists will prove that our brain only serves as a centre, which regulates our bodily functions and limits our awareness within our five senses. The very essence of human consciousness is on another level. There are scientists, who have devoted all their life to the study of the brain and have come to the conclusion that the human memory and consciousness are probably not hiding in the brain.

Three important facts

If in our life we do not want to be constantly embittered and disappointed with all the unfavourable events that are happening to us and over the people we are confronting with, we must consider three important facts.

These are:

1. Everyone must blame itself for all the problems.

2. Everyone does the best according to its level of consciousness.

3. Everything that happens to us is the best for the development of our soul.

If we take these three important facts into account, it will never happen again in our life to be disappointed over someone, or to be afraid of something.

Everyone must blame itself for all the problems

We must be aware, that first we must change ourselves and our actions to our surroundings, and only then the others will change to us. Let us do those things that we can be change by ourselves. It is not useful to expect that someone else is going to do something for us, or things will spontaneously change.

It is also absurd to burden and waste time with things beyond our control. These things have to be taken such as they are.

We should deal with those on which we can influence at any given time. First, however, we can influence on ourselves. But first, we must be willing to change ourselves and our way of thinking. Pythagoras said: "You will find out that people are suffering from things that they have chosen themselves." Buddhists say that the luck must be built, rather than to be waited for it.

If we are not satisfied with things that happen to us in our life, it means, that we acted wrongly in the past and now we are affected by the universal law of cause and effect.

Everyone does the best according to its level of consciousness

Even when somebody was doing something bad, was at that time surely convinced, that it was something useful. In that case, it might be just its own benefit. Such persons are not aware, that with such actions in the long-term harm themselves. The school of life will in the future set them in life situations, where they will receive similar or even more difficult feelings as they caused to others, and so, they will on their own skin experience the pain, that they had done to others.

The purpose of the school of life is to achieve a higher level of consciousness and learn how to deal with other people. It means that if we are good to others, we will be the best to ourselves. Until we don't realize it, so long we are at the same level as animals. They are on such a level of consciousness, that they care only for their current benefits and possess no awareness of good or bad and do not understand that everything in life has its meaning.

If we do not resent the object, a plant or an animal when it hurts us, there is also no need to resent people with a lower level of consciousness when they are bad and hurt us.

When we become aware of the fact that each person makes the maximum of good, depending on his level of consciousness, we will better understand the simple poor old woman who added a log to the stake on which they burnt philosopher Giordano Bruno. We will forgive her, because she was convinced, that she was doing something good. Let us remember the words from the Bible: "Forgive them, they do not know what they do."

Everything that happens to us, is the best for the development of our soul

Everything that happens to us is the maximum good for the development of our soul, but not necessarily for the development of our personality. People can achieve world reputation, power, wealth, influence, but it is not necessary, that it helps them in the development of the soul. It can even be an obstacle for us to develop virtues such as compassion, love, forgiveness, sacrifice, understanding and sacrifice. It is more difficult to achieve these virtues, if we have wealth and the life spares us.

Therefore, our school of life leads us to serious and often to us incomprehensible situations, which enable us the development of certain characteristics. In our material life, we can't understand that they are good for us, but they are necessary for our development and progress. This tells us also the saying from the Bible that it is easier to get a camel through a needle's eye, than for a rich man to come into the kingdom of heaven.

In our life, we are faced with a variety of adverse situations, such as illnesses or accidents, which are in fact the messages that we are doing something wrong.

The first major step towards the healing of a serious disease is to realize, what we have done wrong in the past. For example, the resentment that we are not able to forgive, can lead to a cancer. When we recognize it and change our attitude and feelings, then it will be the right way to full recovery. It is essential to find out what we're doing wrong and try to change it and find the right direction in life.

The fate is hitting us in such way as a shepherd who with his whip directs his sheep on the right path. Everything what happens in our life has a purpose and in all things, we have to see a good purpose.

Our primary mission in life is solving problems

We must believe that we are waiting for salvation, no matter what happens to us. A lot easier for us will be when we become aware of the fact that our primary mission in life is solving problems and overcoming them. Difficulties and problems were prepared by our school of life in order to advance spiritually.

The most of it, what we can do, is to live each day without being angry for every little thing, which is not according to our will.

When we wake up in the morning, do not let us start worry about difficulties and problems which await us again today, but curiously expect what tasks our fate is going to prepare for us. Let us try the best to solve and fulfil them, because of that depends our progress on the scale of our spiritual development and achieving a higher level of consciousness. It works similarly, as in the computer games. The bigger obstacles we managed to solve, the greater our progress and satisfaction was.

We shouldn't take problems as a defeat but as a test and an opportunity that leads us to success and higher spiritual development. If there were no problems and difficulties, there also would be no progress and development. It is hard to imagine a life in the long term, where all our wishes would be granted immediately. Such a life would quickly become bored.

Important is, that we start to control our images of fear and are not bound to them. We must get rid of thoughts of failure. We must believe that we will succeed. With spreading such energy we create circumstances that will help us.

We can accelerate or slow down the progress of our souls, depending on how we respond to different karmic opportunities. Our respond and reaction to the karmic opportunities, and what we have learned from them, determines our new life situations and our destiny in the future. Sometimes, the most difficult people and circumstances open the best opportunities for our advancement.

Let's learn from these short stories!

Struggle

(Author Unknown)

A man found a cocoon of a butterfly. One day a small opening appeared. He sat and watched the butterfly for several hours as it struggled to force its body through that little hole.

Then it seemed to stop making any progress. It appeared as if it had gotten as far as it could and it could go no farther. Then the man decided to help the butterfly, so he took a pair of scissors and snipped off the remaining bit of the cocoon. The butterfly then emerged easily. But it had a swollen body and small, shrivelled wings.

The man continued to watch the butterfly because he expected that, at any moment, the wings would enlarge and expand to be able to support the body, which would contract in time. Neither happened! In fact, the butterfly spent the rest of its life crawling around with a swollen body and shriveled wings. It never was able to fly.

What the man in his kindness and haste did not understand was that the restricting cocoon and the struggle required for the butterfly to get through the tiny opening were nature's way of forcing fluid from the body of the butterfly into its wings so that it would be ready for flight once it achieved its freedom from the cocoon.

The lesson of the story:
Sometimes struggles are exactly what we need in our life. If nature allowed us to go through our life without any obstacles, it would cripple us. We would not be as strong as what we could have been.

Nothing is good or bad!
(By: Lao Tzu)

One day the farmer's only horse jumped the fence and ran away. The villagers came to the farm and said, 'What a great misfortune that your horse has run away.' The farmer said, 'It is neither a fortune nor a misfortune.'

Two or three days later, the horse came back with a dozen wild horses following behind him. The villagers came to him and said, 'It's a great fortune that your horse came back with twelve others.' The farmer replied, 'It is neither a fortune nor a misfortune.'

And then, the following day, his son tried to saddle and ride one of the wild horses, was thrown, and broke his leg. Again, the neighbours came to offer their sympathy for the misfortune. He said, "May be."

The day after that, conscription officers came to the village to seize young men for the army, but because of the broken leg the farmer's son was rejected. When the neighbours came to say how fortunately everything had turned out, he said, "May be."

The lesson of the story:
The farmer was wise enough to know that everything that was happening had a purpose and meaning beyond the simple appearance of the event that had occurred. So many times we are trapped by the emotion of the events in our lives.

.

Tragedy or a Blessing?

(Author Unknown)

Years ago, in Scotland, the Clark family had a dream. Clark and his wife worked and saved, making plans for their nine children and themselves to travel to the United States. It had taken years, but they had finally saved enough money and had gotten passports and reservations for the whole family on a new liner to the United States.

The entire family was filled with anticipation and excitement about their new life. However, seven days before their departure, the youngest son was bitten by a dog. The doctor sewed up the boy but hung a yellow sheet on the Clarks' front door. Because of the possibility of rabies, they were being quarantined for fourteen days.

The family's dreams were dashed. They would not be able to make the trip to America as they had planned. The father, filled with disappointment and anger, stomped to the dock to watch the ship leave - without the Clark family. The father shed tears of disappointment and cursed both his son and God for their misfortune.

Five days later, the tragic news spread throughout Scotland - the mighty Titanic had sunk. The unsinkable ship had sunk, taking hundreds of lives with it. The Clark family was to have been on that ship, but because the son had been bitten by a dog, they were left behind in Scotland.

When Mr. Clark heard the news, he hugged his son and thanked him for saving the family. He thanked God for saving their lives and turning what he had felt was a tragedy into a blessing.

The lesson of the story:
Although we may not always understand, all things happen for a reason. We can't always know what is good or bad for us and our development.

The Thirsty Crow
(Author Unknown)

One hot day, a thirsty crow flew all over the fields looking for water. For a long time, he could not find any. He felt very weak, almost lost all hope. Suddenly, he saw a water jug below the tree. He flew straight down to see if there was any water inside. Yes, he could see some water inside the jug.

The crow tried to push his head into the jug. Sadly, he found that the neck of the jug was too narrow. Then he tried to push the jug to tilt for the water to flow out, but the jug was too heavy.

The crow thought hard for a while. Then, looking around it, he saw some pebbles. He suddenly had a good idea. He started picking up the pebbles one by one, dropping each into the jug. As more and more pebbles filled the jug, the water level kept rising. Soon it was high enough for the crew to drink. His plan had worked!

An Old Mule
(Author Unknown)

There was an old mule. One day accidentally he fell into the farmer's well. The farmer has evaluated the situation and thought to himself, that neither the well nor the old mule was worth the efforts to save them. Thus, he decided to haul dirt to bury the old mule in the well.

So, the farmer called his neighbours and together they started to shovel dirt into the well. The old mule was terrified and hysterical in the beginning. But soon one hopeful idea came to his mind. Every time when a shovel of dirt landed on his back, he would shake it off and step up!

He repeated these words to himself again and again: ,,Shake it off and step up ". This way he could struggle the panic and encourage himself. After some time, the mule had stepped over the well's wall.

Although terribly tired, he was the winner, he saved his own life. He decided to face his adversity positively and not to give up, and thus he won.

The lesson of the stories:
Never give up. Each problem contains the solution. Think and work hard, you may find solution to any problem.

REMEMBER THESE SAYINGS!

The one who can't be angry is the fool. The one who does not want to be is a wise man.

*

Every good thing contains something bad. Every bad thing contains something good.

*

The brave deserves the fair.

*

Cudgels and stones may break my bones, but words will not hurt me.

*

Never expend time thinking about the people which you don't like.

*

Each problem contains the solution at the same time.

*

The time we spend between the beginning and the solution of the problem can serve as a maturing of personality.

*

When one door closes, the other opens.

*

No one is worth of your tears, but that one who is will not cause them.

*

The way is sometimes more important than the final destination.

Rule number 3

Everything you do to others, you are doing to yourself

When you are good to others, you are the best to yourself

Everything you do to others, you are doing to yourself. What would you do if you were absolutely sure that this is true?

People have the feeling, when they give something that they have lost something. This seems to be understandable only, when looking at the short term, because we see only one picture on the film of our life. However, there exist some universal laws based on a certain order and balance.

The situation is similar, as if we were standing in the ocean pushing off water with our hands. More water we push away from ourselves, in larger waves it returns to us to fill the empty space. So, if we want to get something, start first giving something and in increasing waves it will return back.

If you give love, you will receive it back, if you give money you will be repaid, if you give hate, you will get it back.

We must remember the saying that each pronounced curse, after accomplishing the task, returns home. If people were sure that this rule works, they would argue about who pays the restaurant bill and they would gladly give some money to a beggar.

If we received something when we were in need, then we are obliged to repay our "debt" as soon as possible, because on the other side was created the empty space and "the wave can quickly go back".

Whoever takes to that one will be taken away

The rule also works in the other way. Those who take, those will be taken away. Perhaps this can explain quite unintelligible saying from the Bible, which says that those who have will receive more, those who have not will lose even that.

If we suddenly lose something means that it does not belong to us or we don't deserve it, because there are certain unsettled accounts from the past. Our destiny has led us to a specific situation where particular accounts could be settled and we could realize and learn trough these messages that we have done something wrong in the past.

Never expect anything from others and you will never be disappointed

People are often unhappy and disappointed because they expect constant gratitude for all the things which they have offered to certain persons.

Often parents complain how their children received everything from them, but now they are ungrateful and do nothing to return their kindness. People become depressed and say how they were constantly helping their friends and loved ones, but now they don't get anything in return from them.

The solution is very simple. Never expect anything from others and we will never be disappointed. Even, if we help and sacrifice for somebody, do not expect to get a refund. If a repayment happens, it will be only a pleasant satisfaction. Life and destiny will people, whom we had helped, lead to a situation which will further enable them to pay for the services they have received. Our children will further support their children and so on.

Giving is unconditional

True giving is difficult to achieve. Giving is unconditional. True giving is the one when we give to others not to ourselves. Giving someone something with the intention of getting something back in return, is not unconditional giving, but just a repayment for certain services. An old proverb says that what is given is buried in the ground. So, if we don't expect anything in return, we may just be pleasantly surprised when we get something in return. If we expect constant gratitude for all our good deeds, we will be constantly disappointed and miserable. Consequently, this leads to resentment. But resentments are the root cause for the development of diseases, particularly cancerous diseases.

We must learn to forgive

It is very important that in our life we learn to forgive. If we do not forgive, then occurs karmic debt, which is going to effect on our karma or destiny. Consequently, our fate will place us in a situation in which we will have to repay our karmic debts.

What people call fate or God's will is nothing more than the acts of the past which are coming to the realization.

The worst thing for our future and destiny is if we take the revenge for the evil deeds which have been done to us by others in our own hands. We are exposed to the universal law which determines that you will reap what you sow. If we revenge, we will do bad, and bad will return to us. We find ourselves in a vicious circle, from which there is no solution, until it is interrupted by our forgiveness and good deeds.

Everyone will pay for its crimes within a certain period of time

For our revenge will be taken care by a higher power. When somebody hurts us then that one will receive a bad temptation in return. So, there is no need to influence on our destiny by our revenge and consequently call a misfortune upon us.

We just need to wait and watch, because everyone will pay for its crimes within a certain period of time. In the future, such a person will find itself in a situation when it is going to experience similar or even more difficult feelings like those being caused to others. The school of life will bring it to the awareness that it was doing wrong in the past.

As a result, people will improve their reactions and reach a higher level of consciousness. Also, we should not wish anyone bad, because we get it back again. When all people achieve such a level of consciousness, then there will rule on earth peace, order and justice.

Most people are affected by a slight headache more, as if they heard for our death

Often, we put a lot on our reputation and what people think about us. People's words can have a big effect on other's lives. But people like to criticize. A bad opinion of others can quickly hurt us and affect that we feel concerned, incapable and worthless.

The criticism may be an objective, or malicious. Some people criticize others to show themselves more brilliantly. However, the essence of the criticism is helping someone to achieve certain higher level of skills, knowledge or awareness. When the purpose of criticism is unconditional help, then it is going to have real meaning and effect.

If the criticism hurts us too much, we should be aware, that most people are affected by a slight headache more, as if they heard for our death.

Let's learn from these short stories!

Grandpa's story

(Author Unknown)

The old, weak and disabled man lived with his son, his daughter-in-law and his four-year-old grandson. His hands trembled, his look was blurred, and his step hesitated and uncertain.

The family always had a meal together, but the grandfathers' shaky hands and bad vision turned the family ritual into a real nightmare. Pea beads rolled over everywhere, food was sometimes on the ground more than on a plate. When the grandfather reached for the glass with his trembling hands he poured milk on his table, his tablecloth and his ground. It made the son and his wife more and more irritating and angry. For this reason, they placed a special small table in the corner of the kitchen. The grandfather ate alone, while the other family members ate together. Since his grandfather smashed some plates and glasses, his spouses served him in a wooden bowl. Grandpa did not say anything, quietly and humbly ate at her desk, only from time to time on his cheeks glistened tears. The son and daughter-in-law did not find a friendly word for him, and only strict warnings were received from their side when a knife or food from a plate fell on the ground. The four-year-old grandson watched the events quietly.

One evening his father noticed that his son was playing with wooden cubes. He asked him nicely: "What good are you going to do?" He was answered by the child: "Oh, I'm making a small wooden dish for you and Mommy from which you can eat when I am grown up." The child smiled and continued to work. Dad was astonished by his son's words.

50

The same evening, he took his father gently back to the main dining table. The grandfather never ate alone again, but his son and his wife never became upset if a plate fell on the floor or if a glass of drink spilled on the table.

The lesson of the story:
You reap what you sow, everybody gets back good and bad. We teach children by our example.

Mousetrap
(Author Unknown)

There was a farm, where lived farmer John with his wife. They hold pigs, cows and many animals in their farm. Also, there lived a little mouse.

One day the mouse looked through small crack in the wall and accidentally saw how the farmer was opening some package. The mouse was curious what food may it contain and discovered that it was a mousetrap. The mouse was determined to run around the farmyard and warn all the animals regarding the danger.

First, he met the chicken. „There is a mousetrap in the house!" The mouse declared with despair. But the chicken answered with indifference: „It does not concern me, as this is a danger for you, but not for me. It cannot bother me«.

Then the mouse raced to the pig and the cow and told them about the mousetrap. But the pig and the cow where not impressed too. They said that from them there is no reason to worry about this and promised to pray about the mouse. Sad and depressed, the little mouse returned *to the house.*

In the night the farmer's wife heard a sound of a mousetrap. She hurried to see what was in it, but due to the darkness she did not see that it was a poisonous snake, whose tail was caught by the trap. Suddenly the snake bit her. The farmer rushed with her to the hospital. Later, when they returned home, she still had a fever. John remembered that it is good to treat a fever with chicken soup, so he went to his farmyard to bring the main ingredient, the chicken. Whereas his wife's sickness continued and many friends came to visit her. The farmer butchered the pig so he could feed all the visitors. Unfortunately, as time went by, farmer's wife became weaker and weaker and one day she died. Many neighbours, relatives and friends have arrived to the funeral. John had to slaughter the cow to feed all of them.

The mouse has been watching all that was happing with great sorrow.

The lesson of the story:

When someone asks you for help then listen and help him. Do not pretend that this is not your problem and does not matter you, because you do not know how this can be related to your destiny.

Cycle of Evil

(Author Unknown)

There was once a king who was so cruel and unjust that his subjects yearned for his death or dethronement. However, one day he surprised them all by announcing that he had decided to turn over a new leaf. "

No more cruelty, no more injustice," he promised, and he was as good as his word. He became known as the 'Gentle Monarch'. Months after his transformation one of his ministers plucked up enough courage to ask him what had brought about his change of heart.

And the king answered, "As I was galloping through my forests I caught sight of a fox being chased by a hound. The fox escaped into his hole but not before the hound had bitten into its leg and lamed it for life. Later I rode into a village and saw the same hound there. It was barking at a man. Even as I watched, the man picked up a huge stone and flung it at the dog, breaking its leg. The man had not gone far when he was kicked by a horse. His knee was shattered and he fell to the ground, disabled for life. The horse began to run but it fell into a hole and broke its leg. Reflecting on all that had happened, I thought: 'Evil begets evil. If I continue in my evil ways, I will surely be overtaken by evil'. So, I decided to change".

The minister went away convinced that the time was ripe to overthrow the king and seize the throne. Immersed in thought, he did not see the steps in front of him and fell, breaking his neck.

The lesson of the story:
If we are good to others, our good will happen. If we are bad to others, our turn will also come.

A Joke

A doctor, a lawyer, a little boy and a priest were out for a Sunday afternoon flight on a small private plane. Suddenly, the plane developed engine trouble. Despite the best efforts of the pilot, the plane started to go down. Finally, the pilot grabbed a parachute and yelled to the passengers that they better jump, and he himself bailed out.

Unfortunately, there were only three parachutes remaining.

The doctor grabbed one and said, "I'm a doctor, I save lives, so I must live," and jumped out.

The lawyer then said, "I'm a lawyer and lawyers are the smartest people in the world. I deserve to live." He also grabbed a parachute and jumped.

The priest looked at the little boy and said, "My son, I've lived a long and full life. You are young and have your whole life ahead of you. Take the last parachute and live in peace."

The little boy handed the parachute back to the priest and said, "Not to worry Father. The smartest man in the world just took off with my back pack."

The lesson of the story:

Your job doesn't always define you, but being a good human being does.

Remember these sayings!

When you are good to others, you are the best to yourself.

*

You will reap what you sow

*

The smile that you are shining is returning to you. - Indian wisdom

*

Whoever gives the others will be repaid, the one who takes, that one will be taken-Bible

*

Live by the sword, die by the sword

Rule number 4

Seize the day

This moment is basically our only reality

When we observe young children, who have not yet come under the influence of negative thinking, we can see how truly they are living only for the moment. They do not care what happened in the past or worry what will happen in the future. They are living only for the moment. Often, we do not understand them and we consider them for reckless and irresponsible. But adults forget to live for now and enjoying the moment, because they are constantly planning and think about the problems that are still to come.

Although this moment is basically our only reality, we are often burdened with the past which can't be changed.

Hold upright and look forward

A teacher has answered the question on how to ride a bike. He said:" Quite simply, hold upright and look forward." The same applies to our life. If we look back too much, we will lose the balance, because we will be burdened with the past so much, that we will not have time to look ahead and live for the present, which is our only reality. We also must keep moving if we don't want to lose the balance. There is a saying, that we become old when we start dealing with the past more than with the future and present.

We are not fully the owners of our lives

People are very fragile creatures. At this moment, we can be alive and full of energy, the next moment it might happen that we do not live any more. Many young people or parents with small children lost their lives by accidents or illness, although just before that, they had great plans and were full of worries. Later, people can't understand why it happened.

We can't decide about our moment of birth and death. We did not create ourselves. This proves that we are not fully the owners of our lives. Therefore, we must trust to the force which created us and enables our existence.

To this force we should be grateful for every moment of our life. If this force caused and enabled our existence, it also means, that it should also help to solve our problems.

We often forget living the real live

Our daily problems are often insignificant, but we allow them to make our life unhappy and miserable, and we forget living the real live. Our earthly life is short and unpredictable. The only real thing that we have got is this moment, here and now. So use it well!

Whenever we perform a certain activity, we must first ask ourselves whether it really makes us happy, or do we really with this action contribute to our happiness or the satisfaction of others.

Coincidences have the greatest influence on the course of our life

Often people for many events and accidents in the life blame coincidences. We must be aware that coincident play an important role in our life. The biggest coincidences to which we have no influence are in the fact our birth and death. If we carefully observe our lives, we will come to the conclusion that exactly coincidences had the greatest influence on the course of our life. Such as a meeting with our life partners, choosing occupation, meeting with different people, getting a job and various other fortunate or unfortunate events.

Interesting is that Slovenian language contains in the words coincidence and chance (naklucje, slucaj) syllables "key and light". It leads us to the statement that a coincidence could be" the key or light" that guides us.

It is interesting that to some identical twins occurred similar coincidences, even though, they have been living in completely different environments and they did not know each other. They have got life partners with identical names, possessed identical pets with same names, and had the same occupation, the same number of children and so on. Psychologists do not give a precise answer, what impacts on human fate more, or the environment, or genetic material, or certain properties.

Our freedom in the present is our destiny in the future.

Our life can be compared with a journey on a road. It depends on us how and where we are going to travel and how skilfully we will be able to avoid certain obstacles.

The road represents our destiny. It means that there are going to happen also events in our life that are unavoidable for our development. Therefore, we must accept them, because we do not have any influence on them. It is absolutely pointless to burden our life with the future and consequently neglecting our other activities, or our main task, for which we are here.

Our freedom in the present is our destiny in the future. The only influence that we have got in life is the effect on the present moment, so we need to get the best possible use of it and try to find in it the satisfaction and happiness.

When our past burdens us too much, we will have to get rid of it

If we are excessively bonded to the transient and material things, we will be disappointed as soon as we lose them or they go away.

We should be like a balloon in the sky, because wherever the wind takes it, there is its home. When our past, which we are unnecessarily dragging with us, burdens us too much, we will have to get rid of it. Draw a line and start again, without old burdens!

If you are able to correct something from the past, then do it! If the past can't be repaired, not through acts or words, then reconcile it in the spirit. We should be aware that each event is the maximum good for the development of our soul

We can't completely give up, deny and abandon all material things

However, we are living in a material word now and therefore we can't completely give up, deny and abandon all material things.

There are people who devote their lives to spirituality and argue that the material world is irrelevant and untrue and that the spirituality is the only one that counts. They claim that we should completely give up material things. But this is the same as someone living in a spiritual world would deny spiritual things.

We are spiritual beings who are currently having a physical experience. Our mission is to use things that are given to us at this time and the world in which we are currently located in the best possible way for our progress and fortune.

We must try to find the meaning and task of our life

We shouldn't only wait, that something is going to happen in the future. Because such a life is nothing else, but waiting for the death.

We must take care that the others do not live our lives for us. Let us not be like sheep that are led together in a large herd. The others should be an example. Do not blindly follow others, but create your own destiny.

If we do not change and remain at the existing patterns of our behaviour and thinking that make us unhappy, then we are going to live a miserable life.

The sense of our life is undoubtedly not only to survive for the price of our happiness, but trying in the life something else to find the meaning and task of our life and consequently achieve a higher level of spiritual evolution.

Lazy is not the one who does not work, but the one who does not do what he should

A certain person could look very hardworking. However, if someone works hard only for his narrow interests and satisfaction, he might be the subject to the sin of laziness if such a person had avoided his real obligations, such as devoting to his child, or to a neighbour in need.

On the other hand, it is not necessary that someone is a lazy person who is currently not working a lot, if he had done everything that was necessary and urgent.

We are dealing with laziness when we are not doing what we should, no matter how much and what we do.

Let's learn from these short stories!

Enjoy your life at every moment
(Author Unknown)

Once a fisherman was sitting near seashore, under the shadow of a tree smoking his pipe. Suddenly a rich businessman passing by approached him and enquired as to why he was sitting under a tree smoking and not working. To this the poor fisherman replied that he had caught enough fishes for the day.

Hearing this the rich man got angry and said: Why don't you catch more fishes instead of sitting in shadow wasting your time?

Fisherman asked: What would I do by catching more fishes?

Businessman: You could catch more fishes, sell them and earn more money, and buy a bigger boat.

Fisherman: What would I do then?

Businessman: You could go fishing in deep waters and catch even more fishes and earn even more money.

Fisherman: What would I do then?

Businessman: You could buy many boats and employ many people to work for you and earn even more money.

Fisherman: What would I do then?

Businessman: You could become a rich businessman like me.

Fisherman: What would I do then?

Businessman: You could then enjoy your life peacefully.

Fisherman: Isn't that what I am doing now?

The lesson of the story:
You don't need to wait for tomorrow to be happy and enjoy your life. You don't even need to be richer, more powerful to enjoy life. Life is at this moment, enjoy it fully.

Be Happy Now!
(By: Alfred D. Souza)

We convince ourselves that life will be better after we get married, have a baby, then another. Then we're frustrated that the kids aren't old enough and we'll be more content when they are. After that, we're frustrated that we have teenagers to deal with. We'll certainly be happy when they're out of that stage.

We tell ourselves that our life will be complete when our spouse gets his or her act together, when we get a nicer car, are able to go on a nice vacation, when we retire. The truth is, there's no better time to be happy than right now. If not now, when?

Your life will always be filled with challenges. It's best to admit this to yourself and decide to be happy anyway. Alfred D. Souza said: "For a long time it had seemed to me that life was about to begin - real life. But there was always some obstacle in the way, something to be gotten through first, some unfinished business, time still to be served, or a debt to be paid. Then life would begin. At last it dawned on me that these obstacles were my life."

This perspective has helped me to see that there is no way to happiness. Happiness is the way. So, treasure every moment that you have and treasure it more because you shared it with someone special and remember that time waits for no one.

So, stop waiting ... until you finish school, until you go back to school, until you lose ten pounds, until you gain ten pounds, until you have kids, until your kids leave the house, until you start work, until you retire, until you get married, until you get divorced, until Friday night, until Sunday morning, until you get a new car or home, until your car or home is paid off, until spring, until summer, until fall, until winter, until you're off welfare, until the first or fifteenth, until your song comes on, until you've had a drink, until you've sobered up, until you die, until you're born again to decide that.

The lesson of the story:
There is no better time than right now to be happy!

On a Train

(Author Unknown)

A young soldier and his commanding officer got on a train together. The only available seats were across from an attractive young woman who was traveling with her grandmother. As they engaged in pleasant conversation, the soldier and the young woman kept eyeing one another; the attraction was obviously mutual.

Suddenly the train went into a tunnel and the car became pitch black. Immediately two sounds were heard: the "smack" of a kiss, and the "whack" of a slap across the face.

The grandmother thought "I can't believe he kissed my granddaughter, but I'm glad she gave him the slap he deserved." The commanding officer thought, "I don't blame the boy for kissing the girl, but it's a shame that she missed his face and hit me instead." The young girl thought, "I'm glad he kissed me, but I wish my grandmother hadn't slapped him for doing it."

And as the train broke into the sunlight, the soldier could not wipe the smile off his face. He had just seized the opportunity to kiss a pretty girl and slap his commanding officer and had gotten away with both.

The lesson of the story:
Young soldier knew how to seize the day! In the very same way, we must take advantage of every opportunity that comes our way!

Making Sandcastles
(Author Unknown)

A little boy is on his knees scooping and packing the sand with plastic shovels into a bright blue bucket. Then he upends the bucket on the surface and lifts it. And, to the delight of the little architect, a castle tower is created. All afternoon he will work. Spooning out the moat. Packing the walls. Bottle tops will be sentries. Popsicle sticks will be bridges. A sandcastle will be built. Big city. Busy streets. Rumbling traffic.

A man is in his office. At his desk, he shuffles papers into stacks and delegates assignments. He cradles the phone on his shoulder and punches the keyboard with his fingers. Numbers are juggled and contracts are signed and much to the delight of the man, a profit is made. All his life he will work. Formulating the plans. Forecasting the future. Annuities will be sentries. Capital gains will be bridges. An empire will be built.

Two builders of two castles. They have much in common. They shape granules into grandeurs. They see nothing and make something. They are diligent and determined. And for both the tide will rise and the end will come.

Yet that is where the similarities cease. For the boy sees the end while the man ignores it. Watch the boy as the dusk approaches. As the waves near, the wise child jumps to his feet and begins to clap. There is no sorrow. No fear. No regret. He knew this would happen. He is not surprised. And when the great breaker crashes into his castle and his masterpiece is sucked into the sea, he smiles. He smiles, picks up his tools, takes his father's hand, and goes home.

The grownup, however, is not so wise. As the wave collapses on his castle he is terrified. He hovers over the sandy monument to protect it. He blocks the waves from the walls he has made. Salt-water soaked and shivering he snarls at the incoming tide. "It's my castle," he defies. The ocean need not respond. Both know to whom the sand belongs...

The lesson of the story:
We all build castles in the sand. Nothing will last forever. We must learn from children. Go ahead and build, but build with a child's heart. When the sun sets Salute the process of life and go home.

Remember these sayings!

A wise man lives every day a new life.

*

If you everywhere, you're nowhere.

*

Today is the day, which you have yesterday worried about.

*

When you do not know what to do, do what follows.

*

Do not deal with is the things that you can't change, take these things as they are.

*

We are old when we have with the past more joy than with the present and future.

*

Our freedom in the present is our destiny in the future.

*

Our life is a reflection of our previous decisions.

*

Our task is not to try to figure out what awaits us in the hazy distance, but in trying to do what is in all clarity located directly at hand.

Rule number 5

All I need I carry with me

How rich are you?

Rich is the one who is independent of the society and state, even richer is the one who is satisfied with his wealth, but the richest is the one who acquires wealth, he can always carry with him. Even to the other world. Like a magnet which attracts the same things regardless of location.

We are becoming slaves of our work

People need very little for their life. We need something to eat, a roof over our head and heat when it is cold. If this is converted into money, we do not need large sums.

However, we set the criteria for wealth quite differently. It happens that we work hard from morning till night and spend whole days at work. Consequently, we are becoming slaves of our work. We are burdened with various problems, private or official. Our main goal in life is becoming the accumulation and maintenance of material goods. It is no longer possible for us to leave this vicious circle, or we do not even think for a moment that we are not living right. The fact is, that the more material goods we possess, the more things we need to maintain and take care of them.

Money should be the means to achieve certain goals and not a goal

We forget on those things that are the most important in our life. We forget to ask ourselves whether we are in this situation happy and satisfied. Are we willing to change it? We are afraid to jump from this fast train and take time to stop and look up at the beautiful nature that surrounds us.

The success of our life should not be measured by accumulated material goods, but the happiness which we are shining to the outside and into the interior of our essence, therefore, the spiritual goods.

It's nothing bad if we possess certain material wealth or different things that make life easier for us and bring us positive momentary pleasures. The problem arises when we become slaves of money and work. Money should be the means to achieve certain goals and not a goal.

Let's compare the modern civilized people with primitive tribes, which can find in their environment everything to survive. Who is richer then? Those who are forced to work extremely hard all day for the cost of certain personal freedom, or those who caught and gather all the necessary food and live in harmony with nature, which gives them everything they need.

For everything must be paid a certain price

It also does not make sense to look with envy to the neighbors who have got a better car, a bigger house or a higher income. Everything is relative. We can't compare ourselves with others, because everybody must learn different life lessons, according to his school of life. For everything must be paid a certain price.

What helps someone if he earns much more than you, but at the end of the month remains him less than you, or is even in debt, because he has more costs because of his lifestyle. Even more important of that what we possess at the end is, what was the price for certain material goods, we have gained. Probably, there is health, more free time, current tranquility and satisfaction more valuable than material wealth.

Let's start making decisions

To achieve happiness, we need to get rid of all unnecessary clutter to which we are excessively attached in our life and makes us to feel miserable and unhappy. For this we need courage and determination.

Let's start making decisions. Any decision in the long term leads us to the goal, only the way is different. Therefore, we don't need to blame ourselves, that we had made a wrong decision. In life, it is also necessary to take risks. Sometimes, the greatest risk is, that we risk nothing. Any decision to change something in our life can bring a better position, a better job, a better partner, better disposition etc.

Although something looks bad at the certain moment, but it might turn out to be good in the long term. Often, we excessively get involved and insist on things, although it would be better to let them flow, or get rid of them.

Get rid of everything that makes us unhappy

We can get rid of everything that makes us unhappy, even supposing that at the moment it seems to be impossible. If this is not done in time, it may later cause consequences which will be much more unpleasant or even tragic.

However, if we in the life replace negative features, such as fear, passion and ignorance into positive such as courage, moderation, wisdom we will be able to solve all our problems and redirect the destiny in our favor.

Some examples of excessive attachment which might burden our life and we can get rid of it:

Get rid of the unsatisfied job.
Let us be willing to change our work that makes us unhappy and start with something else. Let's reduce our obligations, even for the price of lower income or position. It is pointless to insist on long term job and work in the environment, which is suffocating and killing us, although we have a feeling that it gives us security.

Always we must ask ourselves whether the income and material goods, which we get, are worth more than our freedom and happiness.

We can get rid of the attachment to material things.
For example, why should we be burdened with costs and worries for an expensive and hard affordable car? Just prefer to buy a cheaper one, which will burden us less.

Always ask yourself if something is really so important and worth to possess, that we invest so much into it. If people get rid of greed and excessive attachment to certain things, they will even easier reconcile themselves with death.

We can get rid of a partner.
Why should we the whole life stay in a relationship, waiting for the tragic destiny, with a person who is making us unhappy? Better for all is to break up the unhealthy and unhappy relationship and start a new life. Let's remember the sentence that who is worth of our tears, will never intend to cause them.

We can get rid of too large concerns for our children.
We should also allow them to make some decisions independently so that they will be able to feel the consequences of their decisions. In that case, they will learn the most. We don't need to be involved in everything and must let them to gain their own experience, which will help them to become independent and responsible.

Excessive projecting of our desires, expectations, patterns, messages of our psyche, that we may even not be aware of, can disable a child on its way, because of its rebellion or due to subordination to the wishes of the parents. Cutting ties with children (not before puberty) means that our children are liberated from our excessive influence and that they can walk on their own path.

Our children are not our property. They are independent persons, worthy of all respect and dignity. Effective parents encourage children's independence and their normal tendency of independence.

Our main task is not that we will enable them protection at every step. No matter what we do, we will not be able to provide them complete protection. Therefore, we must stop worry about that. Our mission is to educate and teach them. We must be aware that everyone has his own fate and that we can't create the fate of other people.

We can get rid of excessive attachment to our parents.

It is not possible, that we will refund them every good thing that they have done for us. We don't need to have a guilty conscience, because we did not fully succeed. We must understand that the development goes forward. We will repay good things on our descendants and so settle our "debts" to our parents.

We can also get rid of the loneliness.

This can be done by helping those who need our help. Very soon we won't have any time to think about our own tragedy, disappointment and loneliness. We can become angels in this life.

We can get rid of fear and anger

We must control our fear and anger. Otherwise they intensify and influence on our good fortune, health and character and make our life awful.

Overcoming fear and anger seems to me so important that I devoted them a special attention in the next chapter.

Let's learn from these short stories!

Wisdom
(Author Unknown)

A long time ago, the old king lived. He called his wise men and said, "I want you to do research and build up the wisdom of all time for me. I would like you to write it in a book for the benefit of future generations." They went to the world and returned after a long search time with twelve large books. The blue king measured them and said, "I trust that in these books there is wisdom of all time, but now they are too large; if you do not sum up the wisdom, people will not want to read." The next time they returned with one thick book and the wise king remarked again, "It's still too long. They returned with one chapter, then one page, then one paragraph, and finally one sentence. The King read it and said, "Yes, that's it!" This is the real wisdom of all time. As soon as people around the world learn this wisdom, we will solve many problems. "The sentence was:" No lunch is free! "

The lesson of the story:
Everything in the life has its price.

Kentucky Fried Chicken
(Author Unknown)

Once, there was an older man, who was broke, living in a tiny house and owned a beat-up car. He was living of $99 social security checks. At 65 years of age, he decides things had to change. So, he thought about what he had to offer. His friends raved about his chicken recipe. He decided that this was his best shot at making a change.

He left Kentucky and travelled to different states to try to sell his recipe. He told restaurant owners that he had a mouth-watering chicken recipe. He offered the recipe to them for free, just asking for a small percentage on the items sold. Sounds like a good deal, right?

Unfortunately, not to most of the restaurants. He heard NO over 1000 times. Even after all those rejections, he didn't give up. He believed his chicken recipe was something special. He got rejected 1009 times before he heard his first yes.

With that one success Colonel Hartland Sanders changed the way Americans eat chicken. Kentucky Fried Chicken, popularly known as KFC, was born.

The lesson of the story:

Persistence is very important. Never give up and always believe in yourself despite of rejection.

The Richest Man in the Valley
(Author Unknown)

A rich landowner named Carl often rode around his vast estate so he could congratulate himself on his great wealth. One day while riding around his estate on his favourite horse, he saw Hans, an old tenant farmer. Hans was sitting under a tree when Carl rode by.

Hans said, 'I was just thanking God for my food.'

Carl protested, 'If that is all I had to eat, I wouldn't feel like giving thanks.'

Hans replied, 'God has given me everything I need, and I am thankful for it.'

The old farmer added, 'It is strange you should come by today because I had a dream last night. In my dream a voice told me, 'The richest man in the valley will die tonight.' I don't know what it means, but I thought I ought to tell you.'

Carl snorted, 'Dreams are nonsense,' and galloped away, but he could not forget Hans' words: 'The richest man in the valley will die tonight.' He was obviously the richest man in the valley, so he invited his doctor to his house that evening. Carl told the doctor what Hans had said. After a thorough examination, the doctor told the wealthy landowner, 'Carl, you are as strong and healthy as a horse. There is no way you are going to die tonight.'

Nevertheless, for assurance, the doctor stayed with Carl, and they played cards through the night. The doctor left the next morning and Carl apologized for becoming so upset over the old man's dream. At about nine o'clock, a messenger arrived at Carl's door.

'What is it?' Carl demanded.

The messenger explained, 'It's about old Hans. He died last night in his sleep.'

The lesson of the story:
It's hard to judge what real fortune is and who is really rich. Definitely rich is the one who is satisfied with his wealth.

The Way God Helps
(Author Unknown)

There was a small village by the river. Everyone lived happily and offered regular prayers at the church. Once during the monsoon season, it rained heavily. The river started overflowing and flood entered the village. Everyone started to evacuate their homes and set out to go to the safe place.

One man ran to the church. He quickly went to the priest's room and told him, "The flood water has entered into our homes and it is rising quickly. And water has also started to enter the church. We must leave the village as in no time it will sink under the water! Everyone has set out to go to the safer place and you must come along". The priest told the man, "I am not an atheist like you all and I have a full faith in God. I trust the God that he will come to save me. I will not leave the church, you may go!" So, the man left.

Soon, the water level started to rise and reached the waist height. The priest climbed on the desk. After a few minutes, a man with the boat came to rescue the priest. He told the priest, "I was told by the villagers that you are still inside the church, so I have come to rescue you, please climb on the boat". But the priest again refused to leave giving him the same reason. So, the boatman left.

The water kept rising and reached to the ceiling, so the priest climbed to the top of the church. He kept praying to the God to save him. Soon the helicopter came, they dropped the rope ladder for the priest and asked him to climb on and get inside the helicopter so they can take him to the safer place. But the priest refused to leave by giving him the same reason again! So, the helicopter left to search and help others.

At last, when the church submerged under the water, the priest drowned. He came to heaven and started complaining, "Oh Lord, I worshiped you for all my life and kept my faith in you! Why didn't you come to save me?!" The God appeared in front of him and with a smile, he said, "Oh mad man, I came to save you three times! I came running to you to ask you to leave for the safest place with other villages, I came with a boat, and I came with a helicopter! What is my fault if you didn't recognize me?!" The priest realized his mistake and asked for forgiveness.

The lesson of the story:

In life, opportunities come. We often fail to recognize them and keep complaining that life didn't give us the opportunity to lead a successful life. Always take every chance you get to make a better life.

Remember these sayings!

The brave will have good fortune.

*

Follow your enthusiasm and the universe will open doors where previously the walls were.

*

If you feel that what you possess, do not fit your needs then you would feel bitter, even when the entire world belonged to you.

*

"I once cursed and cursed because
I had no boots
But only until the day when I, so poor,
I met a man who had no foot."

Rule number 6

Be what you are

Every person is unique in the universe

People are often dissatisfied with their appearance, weight, height and even their capabilities. That hurts them very much and would like to look differently or be something else. Consequently, they become less self-confident, although they have no reason for that. We must understand that every person is unique in the universe and that there is nothing equal to it.

In a world without mirrors we would be perfectly satisfied with our image

Many celebrities became extremely successful, even though their appearance was nothing special. They became famous and successful only because of their work and the various opportunities that had enabled them to achieve success and glory.

It happens, that we stand in front of a mirror and observe and estimate ourselves until we notice something which we are not satisfied with. Then we quickly feel bitter and desperate.

Let's imagine a world without mirrors where we would not know how we look like. In this situation, we would not be burdened with our external appearance and would be perfectly satisfied with our image.

What counts is our activity and work

Some people have also problems respecting people of different races or skin colors. We must respect actions and work of others and not their image or outlook. But it is true, that in certain environments live more people with bad characters, or opposite. The reason is that their school of life put them in similar situations. They are like the students in different classes who need to learn specific lessons.

Beauty is not necessarily universal but in individuality

We must realize that we are spiritual beings and that our material body is mortal and subject to various influences, such as aging, illness or injury. Each of us has a weakness. Each of us is in some way damaged, but exactly those errors make our life interesting and worth. Beauty is not necessarily universal but in individuality. Even the most attractive and beautiful person has got only a limited number of years to show its outer beauty. Over the years, however, the external beauty passes quickly, and henceforth all self-confidence, satisfaction and happiness in which they had wrongly built their personality. Not to mention many cosmetic surgeries, which can extend a short-term satisfaction with the external appearance, but later may have even a worse effect.

Real beauty

Many people are considered by their appearance for attractive and beautiful, but in its inside, can carry the disease, hate and resentment. Who is more beautiful then? They, or persons who are satisfied with themselves and their activities and build their personality on the positive work and thoughts and thus acquire wealth, which is imperishable and can always be carried with them.

If we do what makes us happy, then we know that we are on the right way

Certain things we can't change. Like the bee, which is born as a worker bee, can't become a queen bee. Similarly, we can't change certain things, no matter how constantly we strive to do it.

We must accept that we are born in this specific form and in the given circumstances. It has its own purpose, we just need to find out our mission and do the best within the given possibilities. We can set our own task and so become a creator as well. If we do what makes us happy, then we know that we are on the right way.

Let's learn from these short stories!

A folded letter
(Author Unknown)

One day young Thomas Edison came home and gave a paper to his mother. He told her, "My teacher gave this paper to me and told me to only give it to my mother." His mother's eyes were tearful as she read the letter out loud to her child, "Your son is a genius. This school is too small for him and doesn't have enough good teachers for training him. Please teach him yourself."

Many years after Edison's mother had died, Edison had become one of the greatest inventors of the century. One day he was going through the old closet and he found a folded letter which was given to him by his teacher for his mother. He opened it. The message written on the letter was, "Your son is mentally ill. We can't let him attend our school anymore. He is expelled."

Edison became emotional reading it and then he wrote in his diary, "Thomas Alva Edison was a mentally ill child whose mother turned him into the genius of the century.

The lesson of the story:
In each person, we can find hidden potentials. The proper motivation can help to change our destiny.

The Cracked Pot

(Author Unknown)

A water bearer in India had two large pots, each hung on each end of a pole which he carried across his neck. One of the pots had a crack in it, and while the other pot was perfect and always delivered a full portion of water at the end of the long walk from the stream to the master's house, the cracked pot arrived only half full.

For a full two years, this went on daily, with the bearer delivering only one and a half pots full of water in his master's house. Of course, the perfect pot was proud of its accomplishments, perfect to the end for which it was made. But the poor cracked pot was ashamed of its own imperfection and miserable that it could accomplish only half of what it had been made to do.

After two years of what it perceived to be a bitter failure, it spoke to the water bearer one day by the stream. "I am ashamed of myself, and I want to apologize to you". The bearer asked, "Why? What are you ashamed of?" The pot replied, "For these past two years I am able to deliver only half of my load because this crack in my side causes water to leak out all the way back to your master's house. Because of my flaws, you don't get full value for your efforts".

The water bearer felt sorry for the old cracked pot, and in his compassion, he said, "As we return to the master's house, I want you to notice the beautiful flowers along the path." As they went up the hill, the old cracked pot took notice of the sun warming the beautiful wild flowers on the side of the path, and this cheered it somewhat. But at the end of the trail, it still felt bad because it had leaked out half its load, and so again it apologized to the bearer for its failure.

The bearer said to the pot, "Did you notice that there were flowers only on your side of your path, but not on the other pot's side? That's because I have always known about your flaw, and I took advantage of it. I planted flower seeds on your side of the path, and every day while we walk back from the stream, you've watered them. For two years I have been able to pick these beautiful flowers to decorate my master's table. Without you being just the way, you are, he would not have this beauty to grace his house."

The lesson of the story:

Each of us has our own unique weaknesses. We're all cracked pots. In this world, nothing goes to waste. You may think like the cracked pot that you are inefficient or useless in certain areas of your life, but somehow these imperfections can turn out to be a blessing in disguise.

The Peacock and the Crow
(Author Unknown)

A crow lived in the forest and was absolutely satisfied in life. But one day he saw a swan. "This swan is so white," he thought, "and I am so black. This swan must be the happiest bird in the world."

He expressed his thoughts to the swan. "Actually," the swan replied, "I was feeling that I was the happiest bird around until I saw a parrot, which has two colors. I now think the parrot is the happiest bird in creation." The crow then approached the parrot. The parrot explained, "I lived a very happy life until I saw a peacock. I have only two colors, but the peacock has multiple colors."

The crow then visited a peacock in the zoo and saw that hundreds of people had gathered to see him. After the people had left, the crow approached the peacock. "Dear peacock," the crow said, "you are so beautiful. Every day thousands of people come to see you. When people see me, they immediately shoo me away. I think you are the happiest bird on the planet.

"The peacock replied, "I always thought that I was the most beautiful and happy bird on the planet. But because of my beauty, I am entrapped in this zoo. I have examined the zoo very carefully, and I have realized that the crow is the only bird not kept in a cage. So, for past few days, I have been thinking that if I were a crow, I could happily roam everywhere.

The lesson of the story:

We often make unnecessary comparison with others and become sad. We don't value what we are and what we have. This all leads to the vicious cycle of unhappiness. Learn to be happy in what you have, instead of looking at what you don't have. There will always be someone who will have more or less than you have. Person who is satisfied with what he/she has, is the happiest person in the world.

The Chicken

(Author Gary Barnes)

Once upon a time, there was a large mountainside, where an eagle's nest rested. The eagle's nest contained four large eagle eggs. One day an earthquake rocked the mountain, causing one of the eggs to roll down the mountain to a chicken farm located in the valley below. The chickens knew that they must protect and care for the eagle's egg, so an old hen volunteered to nurture and raise the large egg.

One day, the egg hatched and a beautiful eagle was born. Sadly, however, the eagle was raised to be a chicken. Soon, the eagle believed he was nothing more than a chicken. The eagle loved his home and family, but his spirit cried out for more. While playing a game on the farm one day, the eagle looked to the skies above and noticed a group of mighty eagles soaring in the skies. "Oh," the eagle cried, "I wish I could soar like those birds."

The chickens roared with laughter, "You cannot soar with those birds. You are a chicken and chickens do not soar."

The eagle continued staring at his real family up above, dreaming that he could be with them. Each time the eagle would let his dreams be known, he was told it couldn't be done. That is what the eagle learned to believe. The eagle, after time, stopped dreaming and continued to live his life like a chicken. Finally, after a long life as a chicken, the eagle passed away.

The lesson of the story:
You become what you believe you are. So, if you ever dream of becoming an eagle, follow your dreams, not the words of a chicken. Be what you are, find yourself and be it.

Remember these sayings!

Find yourself and be yourself.

*

Nobody on the earth is like you.

*

Each makes its own fortune.

*

Peace comes from within, do not seek it outside.

POSITIVE AFFIRMATIONS

We always give commands to our subconscious mind in the affirmative form. Our subconscious mind can easily overlook and miss the words like: no, not, don't. The subconscious mind, like a dog, does not understand the word "not". If we say to the dog" we are not going for a walk" it will hear the word "walk". Our subconscious mind could understand the sentence "I'm not ill" like "I'm ill". The correct affirmation is "I am healthy".

Consider the fact, that the disease did not occur overnight, the same way our body also uses its time for healing.

Many positive affirmations can be found in the books of Louise L. Hay.

A good affirmation is:

- Personal,
- positive and in the present time,
- visual,
- emotional,
- not repeated endlessly,
- the attention must be paid that from the wishes no one is deprived,
- affirmation should include the expectation of a positive solution, not a request

Seize the day:

Today is the best day of my life.
The past against me has no more power. Thoughts in the present moment create my future.
Every day brings me a new opportunity.
Today I am not angry at any person, place or thing. I'm calm.
I can deal with all situations.
I am in a good mood and I look forward to every day of my life.

Think positively:

Everything is fine. Everything is going in my best. Only the best comes from this situation. I'm safe.
My body does everything to be completely healthy.
My happy thoughts help my body to restore health. I am resistant to...
My good thoughts are changing the world around me.
My life is simple and easy.
Throughout my life I know that I am safe.

What does not destroy me makes me stronger:

I get all the help from various sources when I need it.
When I make a mistake, I realize that this is just a part of the learning process.
Law of attraction brings into my life just good.
Life supports me in all possible ways.
Each obstacle is a step towards the goal.
Easily I control every situation.

Everything you do to others, you are doing to yourself:

I can learn something from each person who is present in my life.
The fact, that we live together, has the hidden purpose.
Life is very simple. All that we give will be refunded.

All I need I carry with me:

My income is constantly growing. I become wealthy at every step.
Life with a large abundance takes care of all my needs. I trust life.
My wealth comes from everywhere and from everyone.
No matter where I am, there is only the infinite abundance, infinite wisdom, infinite harmony and infinite love.
A perfect job is waiting for me and now I meet it.
I find reason for joy in each little thing.
All doors are open to me.
I am totally successful in everything I start. I have faith in myself and my abilities.

Be what you are:

I am successful at every step.
I am discovering talents, which I did not know that I have.
I am always in touch with my creative source.
I know I can create miracles in my life.
I'm a creature who enjoys the fullness of life.
I have the inner strength to realize all the wishes.

FEAR, ANGER, ENVY

"Enjoy and embrace your challenges because these are your life lessons."

Fear

One of the main tasks in life is how to overcome fear

It has evolved as a positive and useful emotion which helps living beings to avoid direct objective threats that can't be overcome, such as fire, dangerous animals, water etc.

Now, it usually manifests itself as a continuous and excessive fear of things that can't be changed and to which we have no influence. We fear for our children, of losing a job, illness, war, death, the unknown. But in fact, these all are the things that are destined for us, because of our previous actions and they are good for our development and progress of our souls, although we are not currently aware of it. The fear means that we don't trust the natural flow of life.

In fact, we are afraid of changes. But exactly the changes are the only constant in life as said the writer Isaac Asimov. This applies not only to life, but for the entire universe. If things aren't changing and moving, the whole universe would collapse.

Although we fear the changes, we all basically want them. The biggest punishment for people is the lack of changes. But on the other hand, we are afraid of them. When we are exposed to a minimum of changes, like a prison cell, it will be the greatest suffering for us. So, it shouldn't be so hard for us, to get to the level that we are not going to be afraid of changes and become brave enough to act. Changes are sometimes very painful, but they teach us that that we can become stronger.

Especially the fear of death is one of the most burdensome things. Because we are aware, that we will not be able to avoid it. It's not just the fear of losing material things, friends, relatives and all our memories, but also the fear of losing our consciousness and personality and the fear of falling into total darkness and absence.

There are two types of people.

The first types of people are those who believe in the afterlife and the continuation of our consciousness in some different way. They even expect the expansion of our consciousness, liberation from the pain and the senses which can hinder and deceive us. They also expect a judgment for their deeds that might befall them.

Definitely, such people in any case don't need to be afraid of the death, because they are expected to continue their lives in some new form. Consequently, there is a possibility that they will also meet with the others, settle unfinished bills, because material death is not the end. In that case, we are spiritual beings who currently have physical experience in our current form. These people can only fear of a judgment for their bad deeds, which can be avoided by doing good deeds in their life.

Another type of people believes that dead is definite end of existence. Namely, they will become forever a complete nothingness, without any consciousness.

In fact, those who do not believe in the afterlife also have nothing to fear, because they will not have to pay for all bad deeds in their life. This sounds even more illogical, because in their lives they can commit crimes without any consequences and it might happen that they will never be responsible for their bad deeds.

From a philosophical perspective, there are two options.

The first option is, that in the universe everything is eternal and infinite, variable and repeatable. In this case also our life and consciousness can be eternal and can be repeated in some different form.

The second option is, that everything has its end. This means that it might also be, that the death has an end and is not eternal and final.

Even scientists explain that the universe can't be deprived of anything and nothing can be added. Everything can only vary from one form to another. They also conclude that a complete nothingness can't exist at all. Also, nothing must be something.

It has been said that those who do good deeds can't end bad. No exercises can help us to eliminate fear until we realize the essence of our fear. We must change our attitudes to it and consequently change our patterns of thinking and behaviour. We must start to trust the natural flow of life.

Anger

It is essential, to get rid of our anger

Anger occurs when events are not taking place according to our expectations. This happens in our life very often. However, from each our outbreak of anger, there are no practical benefits. With anger we only show our own vulnerability with which we do not want to face.

We must be aware that no one has just the luck. We are constantly faced with problems and difficulties. They are in fact school lessons in our development to a higher level of consciousness that separates us from the animals. If there were no problems or challenges, our lives would be dull and no progress and development would happen.

If we don't begin to control our everyday anger, it will only intensify and influence on our well-being, health and character, until our life will become unbearable.

With anger and swearwords, we attract curses to ourselves and others. Namely, we are creating so-called circle of evil. The angrier we are the more negative energy we create and the more negative forces we attract. Consequently, this could create/ they help to create new negative events. Evil forces like troubles, because they are fed and powered with our negative energy. We urgently must stop our anger.

We begin stopping it by using a similar method as for negative thinking. Anger is nothing more than an explosion of the negative emotions that are the result of frequent negative thoughts. Let's start consistently mark and count our tantrums. For each outburst of anger determine a penalty. For example, we throw a coin in a box. Quickly we will have accumulated a surprisingly large sum of money. Let us call it a punishment for anger and dedicate it to a good purpose for someone else. As soon we become aware of tantrums, they will begin to diminish with time.

Mainly we are angry due to the events and people which are not in accordance with our expectations, or because we have lost something or we did not get something.

When we lose something or we didn't get what we expected, this simply means, that it doesn't belong to us. The same as the universe can't be deprived of anything and nothing can be added, the same in the long term, we can't get something or lose something if it does not belong to us, or we do not deserve it. The fact is, that through our actions in the past, we haven't done enough, or haven't learned enough yet, to deserve it. We simply must accept it, because no anger will help. We can correct this with actions in the future. It also doesn't make any sense to be angry, because we can't know and judge whether something is good or bad for us. In the future we can recognize that something is good for us, although we had been once angry because of that.

If we are angry on other people, then we have to recall, that everyone makes maximum good depending on his level of development. This means that for such a person it is difficult to act otherwise, because it has not yet reached a higher level of knowledge and awareness. It makes no sense to be angry on such a person, we can only help it.

When we get mad due to sudden events that are not developing in accordance with our expectations, then we must immediately stop, and let us take time for calming down and thinking it over.

I call it the method of my service technician. At work he is daily faced with various problems that the average person would quickly bring into a rage. He holds to his effective rule that never gets angry. When he faces with the problem, he stops working, sits down and thinks about the possible solution of the problem. So, the efficient order before the outbreak of anger is: stop, sit down, think about and calm down, find a solution.

Envy

Stop your envy

Often, we wonder why some people have a lot of money and property. We can't understand why a football player or a pop star earns in a week more than a professor, a doctor or a scientist in a year. It seems to us unfair and we have the feeling that we have never been at the right time in the right place. Mostly we envy such people and want to be in their place.

We need to consider that everybody is with the reason exactly at the place where it should be. Each one has its own school of life and must learn exactly those lessons that are the best for its development.

Judging other people by the current financial or life situation, without considering a longer period of time, may be similar of being envious on a man who could afford to buy a ticket for the Titanic.

The wealth of the world is distributed fairly. The wealth has got that one who deserves it. But it is true that a certain situation can quickly change. The rich can suddenly lose much more than the poor. The loss for a rich man may be quite more painful and more difficult to undergo. It's also difficult to recognize what real wealth is.

It is also important how much wealth and fortune has got someone in reserve due to its former good works. The most important is, how many people have been made happy and satisfied by our actions and deeds. Someone can make happy and overjoy millions of people, or make their life easier, with their music, plays, works of art and inventions. It is no wonder that such a person deserves wealth. You need to ask why you do not deserve it, what you are doing wrong and what you can change.

Everything has its price. Everything must be repaid. Therefore, it is also difficult to obtain wealth by gambling. First, because taking money without giving anything can't bring the gains in the long term. Secondly, such an activity gives very little satisfaction and happiness to others. But it can make profit to the owners of casinos, because their activity, like amusement parks, allows satisfaction to the masses of people.

THE SENSE OF LIFE

"Life is like riding a bicycle. To keep your balance, you must keep moving." (Albert Einstein)

The meaning of life

Every person sooner or later comes to the point when it asks itself what is the meaning of life. Although we often, due to constant every day pressures, the fast tempo of life and an excessive obsession with materialism can't find the time to deal deeply with the question of the meaning of life. When observing the various primitive beings, we get the feeling that their life has no real meaning at all. They are living a short life in which they are mainly looking for food and reproducing. However, similar can be said for most people. Some highest form of intelligence might also consider human life for completely irrelevant without any sense. Alike the most primitive creatures we are born, we strive for food, territory, material things, we multiply and then die.

The basic meaning of life, or existence should logically be the same for all living creatures.

It is difficult to judge whose life has a meaning and whose does not. There is no general rule which could determine that somebody lives a life that has a real meaning and is worth more than from the others.

People find different meanings in life like: serving to God, helping others, taking care for others, changing the world, teaching others, becoming successful, accumulating possessions, gaining wealth, achieving spiritual progress, creating, conquering...

But there is a difference between the meaning of life and sense of existence.

The fact is, that there is no special sense of existence at all. It is already the existence by itself in the mighty eternity and infinity of cosmos. The actions enable us to bear easier the eternity.

The basic sense of material life is to get the experience of transience. Everything else we can only imagine and determine by ourselves. We are namely the spiritual creatures who are currently achieving material experience.

With our activities and with our creative ability, we have the opportunity to influence on ourselves and the world around us. As a result, our existence can be improved and facilitated. However, we must be careful, that our activities do not hurt the others, because consequently according to the law of karma we hurt ourselves.

THE SELF-HEALING METHOD

We must be aware that there are no incurable diseases.
The human spirit, our consciousness, sub consciousness, thoughts, energy, have an influence on our body. Evidence for that is a number of miraculous and spontaneous cures over which official medicine has already given up. For example, cancerous cells have completely disappeared, because the patient believed in the medicine or had enough faith in God's help.

In fact, the evidence of the influence of psyche and thought is already a disease in itself, because there is always psychic stress, fear or negative thinking and expectation in the background. Therefore, it is vice versa. The correct thinking and proper lifestyle, will also help to cure the disease completely.

When facing a severe illness, we follow the following steps:

We accept the disease and consider it as an indicator that we are on the wrong path and that we are not doing something right in our life and we need to change it. If we do not change it the disease might return, even after healing.

1. **Let us forgive everyone** and correct the things that we hurt the others, as far as we can. We can also make a vow what we will do when we are healed, or what we will change in our lives for the better.

2. **Immediately begin to change the mental patterns from negative to positive.** (I'm healthy and I feel healthy, I receive health from all sources...). All cells in the body are replaced with new ones within two months. Therefore, it is only necessary to enter the information in our sub consciousness, so that they again will be properly restored, sorted and can form healthy body organs. The word "information" has got its origin in Latin with the meaning "to make a form".

3. **We visualize our cure.** We present a precise scene in our future, how we are healthy again (e.g. the doctor informs us that cancer cells have disappeared, a scene when you are healthy and happy again with your family, or in your workplace ...) *I have never experienced greater happiness than when my wife received the message that she does not have cancer anymore and my visualization was fulfilled.*

4. **We ask for the help our creator** (the power that has enabled our existence), the energies around us which can't be perceived with our five senses, our sub consciousness, our spiritual guides and invisible souls...That all will lead us to the circumstances, people, information, situations, coincidences which will enable our healing in the shortest possible time. We thank for all our requests, as if we had already received them.

5. **We start to insert positive vibrations into all food and drink** before ingesting it. We do this by focusing our mind on food in order to give us health and strength. Throughout

history we know the blessing of food. Even recent research has found that mental information affects the water.

Remember these sayings!

Happiness is the path to the health.

*

„Don't be excessively concerned about health – that itself is sickness." Sadguru

*

"Because of your faith, it will happen." Jesus

*

"We never have a true idea of our health value until we lose it."

*

The secret of health for both mind and body is not to mourn for the past, nor to worry about the future, but to live the present moment wisely and earnestly. Budha

*

A healthy outside starts from the inside.

EPILOGUE

Wherever is your consciousness, there is your home

Currently, we consider for the only reality what is presented by our brains. In our dreams we consider the dream world for reality. Under the influence of hypnosis, drugs or brain damage is an altered state of consciousness again a reality which we believe. However, we all know that our senses are limited and can mislead us. Often people say that they believe only what they see. However, they can't see even the air they breathe and keeps them alive.

If we had the ability to see and perceive everything, life would lose its meaning and become incredibly boring. It's like to play a game of cards with cards faced up.

We do not know what the true reality is. Hindus say that our world is an illusion. Some contemporary researchers also claim that the whole universe could be a huge hologram.

Let's imagine that we can put our consciousness into a computer program where is created a new virtual world. In this virtual world we would be sure that the world we experience and perceive is completely true and the only and true reality.

This theme is shown in the film Matrix. Earlier it was debated by Plato in Allegory of the Cave in his work The Republic. Plato created a scenario which shows mankind the true picture of an imaginary world.

The idea is that even if someone knew the truth that there is a different world that is more real than that which we perceive, people would not believe him. He would not be able to convince them that what they perceive as reality are only shadows of another real world.

Maybe we also blindly believe our senses and current beliefs.

Never say, I believe only what I see, because you're embarrassing all blind people.

Just be and act well. There is a reason to be exactly where you are. You must find out what your life lesson is.

INDEX

CPSIA information can be obtained
at www.ICGtesting.com
Printed in the USA
LVHW081611010620
657133LV00034B/2476